MW01134492

How To L
Self-Confidence in Just 30 Days

25 Things Parents Can Do to
Teach Your Child Unstoppable
Self-Confidence

Denny Strecker

Copyright © 2017 by DennyStrecker.com, Inc.

Would you like to get free updates and some *COOL* gifts?
I am constantly working on new skills and adding techniques to my toolkit.
When I add something to this book, you will get it for free. Just visit:

http://DennyStrecker.com/confidencebook-bonus

ENDORSEMENTS AND ACCOLADES

"Your mentorship has improved Logan's shyness, his physical fitness, his confidence, and every other aspect that karate improves kids. But you also improved me. I learn so much watching and listening to you. I gained so many techniques on how and what makes Logan tick. You are making me a better father (I didn't think it was possible). Have a great weekend and thank you!"

Michael Dyja (Sterling Heights, Mi)

"We are so happy Cassie decided to try out Karate! It's been 5 months since she started and she's gained so much confidence and self esteem in that time. Cassie has always and still is the smallest/shortest in her grade and at times feels out of place and defeated. Your class has given her a sense of self worth and she shines bright every time she sets foot in class. This class has also taught her respect on a deeper level,which as a mom, I'm super impressed how she will still say "Yes, ma'am!" at home. Lastly, your special dedication to each student and their family is extraordinary-you always greet the whole family with a smile and genuinely care about your students! You pay attention to every detail from your ultra clean smelling karate studio to helping families with helpful parenting info (weekly email topics, podcasts, student weekly challenges, and parent night-outs), and of course creating a fun interactive karate instruction!! In our book you're A#1!!"

Karri Lido (Troy, Mi.)

"Zach is autistic and social situations are always a struggle.Karate has pushed Zach far outside his comfort zone. He now has more confidence because of this.

You have been a real blessing to us. You've made a big difference in his life. Thank you."

Donald Kolosick (Roseville, Mi.)

How To Double Your Child's Self-Confidence in Just 30 Days

"In the last 2 months Hunter has been in karate, I have seen such an improvement with him not only with behavior at school but at home also. Best therapy for him. He had Belt Testing tonight and has already ranked up to a yellow-white belt. He is so proud of himself!!!"

Kristie Jorah (Madison Heights, Mi.)

"...I only can say thank you a thousand of times to Denny Strecker because more than a business he do care sooooo much about the kids and he always trust in Keven! Thank you because you believe not only in Keven you believe in all the kids and help them to believe in themselves."

Doriel Garcia (Pontiac, Mi.)

"...Dakota was having a lot of problems in school with being able to stay focused, discipline, and some other behavior issues.

The teachers and principle suggested to us that we should take him to see a doctor to possible medicate him in order to help him stay on track. As a parent, I do not believe any of us want to medicate our children as a first step to helping them 'fix' their issues. We decided to do some research and found that a lot of kids that are struggling with focus, discipline, and behavior issues were enrolled in Karate. So as a mom, I did my research and found Denny Strecker.

When Dakota went back to school that fall, we were approached by the principal and asked us what did we do over the summer as the change in Dakota was immediately noticed by all!

Thank you for all your help and everything you do!"

Denise DeGolyer (Sterling Heights, Mi.)

WHY DID I WRITE THIS BOOK?

I wrote this book because for the past 25 years I have had parents bring their shy and introverted children who were struggling at school with grades and having a hard time fitting in and making friends. Week after week, I was able to help each child develop their confidence AND do better in school. Then, I started hearing stories from parents.

"I wish my sister lived closer because her kids NEED your program."

"I have a co-worker who is at their wits end with their child, but they live on the other side of town."

I started to hear this more and more and so I thought to myself, how can I help the families that need my information, but are not in my area? Write a book...!

I would like to thank all the people who helped me along the way and to making this book possible:

Melody Shuman who is the creator of the SKILLZ program and has been a mentor to me for over 20 years.

All the parents who have enrolled their children in my program over the years and allowed me to work with them and learn the best way to help children.

And most of all, to my parents who have always supported me and been my biggest fan!

WHY SHOULD YOU READ THIS BOOK

This book will help you...

Become a better parent by teaching you the tools I use every day with great success to help children..

In the next 30 days, you are going to see your child's confidence soar with my easy to implement techniques. You are going to feel so much joy watching your child grow and develop that you will be upset that you had not done this sooner. **<u>Don't be!</u>** These techniques have been reserved for my clients only so you did not know that you did know this stuff. This book will fix that.

Your child is going to enjoy all the benefits of having confidence and see all kinds of doors open to them. When your child has a good level of confidence, they will:

- Be very likeable and have plenty of friends
- Be able and willing to face new challenges
- Be willing to take on roles of leadership
- Be happier in their daily life
- Take pride in their accomplishments
- Work harder to earn the things they want
- And so much more....!!!!

Sound like a dream come true? Well, let's get started and in just 30 short days you will see what I have seen hundreds of times with the children I work with in my program.

TABLE OF CONTENTS

CHAPTER 1. TEACH DON'T JUST EXPECT

"At the end of the day, the most overwhelming key to a child's success is the positive involvement of parents." - **Jane D. Hull**

MAKE YOUR BED!

Carol was the mom of Tommy, one of my seven year old Yellow Belts. She was a good mom. She was involved in all of Tommy's activities and made it a point to ask questions to make sure he did not miss something. Carol was sitting in my office telling me how frustrated she was that Tommy was not able to make his bed. Her reasoning was, "He is **SEVEN YEARS OLD**! He should know how to make his bed!!" To which I simply replied, "Have you ever shown him how to do it?"

DON'T JUST EXPECT THINGS

As a Parent, you need to teach their child how to doing anything, you can't just expect them to do it. Watching parents day in and day out interacting with their children, it got me thinking about this issue. Too often, parents expect their child to be able to do something without the proper education on how to do it.

Whenever you start a new job, you always have an orientation. In a lot of instances when you go to a new school, there is an orientation that gets you acclimated with what is going to happen, what is expected and where you are supposed to be. There really isn't any type of orientation for children. The kids grow up and parents and grandparents just expect their children to know a lot of the rules in life. That is not what works. What I hear all the time from parents is,

"They should know how to do this because they are seven years old."

There is no correlation between learning a new skill based on age. A child does not know how to make their bed because they are seven years old. They know how to make their bed because you have taught them how to do it – whatever their age!

What I would like to challenge you with is put an "if" after that "should" and check to see if you are teaching or are you just expecting. At that point it would be you "should" know that your clothes belong in the dirty clothes' basket if I have taught you that is where they go. It is not a matter of telling them once and they know how to do it.

The really cool part, is that this is a universal principle. It applies to adults, to your significant others, your spouse, your co-workers, as well with children. If you start teaching this concept to your children, it is going to give them a leg up in the world. Every time that you use "should" you can think to yourself, "Did I teach them how to do it?" If the answer is, "No, I haven't," then you need to back up and teach them the skill you are interested in seeing them do.

One of the techniques I use when I work with a child is saying to them, "I'm only going to tell you that 10,000 more times." It is a fun thing that I say to let the child know that I am here to help them. I am your mentor. I am your coach. Don't feel bad because you forgot, that is my job to remind you.

Assignment #1

Your first assignment is to make a list of things you want your child to be able to do. Once you have that list, then go over it again and prioritize which items are the most important. Finally, pick **ONE**, and work on it for the next month. If we use the making your bed example, it may go something like this:

Week 1 - Make the bed and have your child
Week 2 - Make the bed by having your child tell you what to do step by step
Week 3 - Watch your child make the bed
Week 4 - Have your child make the bed and have you check it when they believe it is done correctly.

For a podcast that will help you become a Black Belt Parent, visit
http://DennyStrecker.com/confidencebook-bonus

Lots of free examples are in the included as a bonus for buying my book.

How To Double Your Child's Self-Confidence in Just 30 Days

Chapter 2. How To Make Friends

"Walking with a friend in the dark is better than walking alone in the light." -
Helen Keller

George Hides Behind Mom

Terri called me and was incredibly stressed and worried about her son, George. George was a really nice and sweet boy but was painfully shy. At six years old, he did not speak very much to anyone, even extended family members. Terri was afraid that George was going to suffer from this shyness his whole life. This would impact him negatively in all kinds of ways. I asked her to bring George in so I could meet him and see how I could help.

It only took a couple of seconds to see what Terri was worried about when I met them. George hid behind her and did not make any eye contact and definitely did not have anything to say to me.

We sat down and I explained to Terri how to work on the Polite Introduction which would improve his confidence and help him to make friends and would open all kinds of doors in his life. Terri and I practiced a few times and then she practiced it with George. They left with a great plan in place.

About two weeks later, Terri called and said,

"You won't believe what happened. Your idea worked! Today, George made a new friend at school and he couldn't wait to tell me all about it when he got home from school!"

Friends Are Very Important

Teaching your child how to make friends is an incredibly important thing in your child's social development. I don't know of anybody who has ever sat down and said, "Here look, here is a system of five things ..." (which is what I am going to show you in this chapter,) "... to help you make friends." Role play them and put them together with your child. Then they know what to do."

I get parents coming to me saying,

"My child is so shy. My child goes off onto the side of playground and sits by themselves. They never interact."

That just breaks your heart thinking that they are going to be alone like that. This will be the best thing that will help if you have one of those shy kids.

There are 5 steps to the process I teach my students in how to complete a Polite Introduction. Each step is important so make sure you practice this with your child any chance you get. Don't worry about how well they do it right away. Focus on getting them to learn the steps fist. Then, you can work on improvement after they remember each step.

Step #1 - Look the person in eye

It is important to make eye contact with the person so they know you are interested in speaking with them. I have had kids tell me how their feelings got hurt because they tried to speak with someone and were ignored or worse, the person walked away. The trouble is, the person was not being mean, they were focusing on something else and did not hear or see that the child was speaking to them. So by making sure you make eye contact first, you can eliminate this potential problem.

Step #2 - Smile!

It is always amazing to me to see how many people walk around with a frown or even a scowl on their face all day. No one wants to talk to someone who is in a bad mood. So make sure you smile and let the person know you are friendly and excited to speak with them.

As a special note, you have to practice your smile! I ask kids to smile all the time and see some very scary smiles. The kids look down right scary, or like they are in physical pain. It is important to teach them how to smile.

Step #3 - Shake With Your Right Hand

Teach your child how to shake someone's hand properly. Nothing is worse than a "dead fish" handshake which is a limp, weak hand. Just as bad is the "death grip" where you try to squeeze the hand as hard as you can. Kids have to learn that somewhere between these two extremes is what they want to do.

Next, you want to teach your child when is a good time to let go. Have you ever had someone shake your hand for too long? It feels really awkward and leaves a feeling of "ick" with the person you just met. That is never a goal of what we want people thinking after we meet them. Make sure you teach your child this step by practicing it over and over.

BONUS: Here is a fun history fact for you.

We shake with our right hand because in the old days everyone carried a weapon and you learned how to use that weapon with your right hand. By offering your weapon hand to someone, you are saying, "I mean you no harm." because you cannot use your weapon if you are shaking their hand.

This is a fun story the kids love to hear in my classes. Now you can share it with your child too.

Step #4 - Introduce Yourself

The ball is rolling and your child has started off really strong. Now we want them to continue on this strong path and that means in a clear voice, introduce yourself. Simply say, *"Hi, my name is ... What is your name?"*

How To Double Your Child's Self-Confidence in Just 30 Days

Have them keep good eye contact and a pleasant smile.

Your child is almost home and has just one more thing to do.

Step #5 - Listen and Repeat!

The final step will accomplish two great things for your child. First, it will help anchor the person's name in their mind so they will remember it later. Second, it will show the person that you actually are paying attention to what they have said and that you care.

Teaching your child this skill alone is going to give them a great tool, which takes us back to Chapter One about just expecting. Don't expect your child to make friends, be proactive and teach them exactly what to do so they are able and ready to meet people anywhere they go.

Assignment #2

Teaching your child a system to introduce themselves will help improve their confidence in so many ways. Your assignment is to practice this with your child until they have is down AND then have them practice it with other people. Have them do a Polite Introduction with your neighbor, Grandma, their school teacher, their friends and anyone else you see throughout the day.

Advanced Lesson: After your child is able to perform this skill really well, ask them questions about the person they met later on that day. You can ask things like:

"What was their name?"
"Where did you meet them?"
"What color jacket did they have on?"
"What did you like about them?"

These questions will help them improve their short term memory which will benefit them in school AND in life..

For a video that will show you the Polite Introduction and help you become a Black Belt Parent, visit http://DennyStrecker.com/confidencebook-bonus

Lots of free examples are in the included as a bonus for buying my book.

CHAPTER 3. REMIND YOUR CHILD OF PAST VICTORIES AND ACCOMPLISHMENTS

"Patience, persistence and perspiration make an unbeatable combination for success." - **Napoleon Hill**

DON'T GIVE UP BECAUSE OF ONE BUMP IN THE ROAD

Maximus is a super kid who has been in my program for several months. He is really kind and very enthusiastic every time I see him. One day in class, he was being a little lazy so I lightly kicked his backside to get him moving a little quicker, just as I have done hundreds of times with the kids in my class. Well, he did not like that one bit. He decided I was a terrible person and he did not ever want to come to another class. The grandparents called to tell me about this and then let me know about some of the history behind why this did not go well with him. I understood why Max felt the way he did and explained how I would correct the situation the next time Max came to class.

Max reluctantly came back to class and I apologized if I hurt his feelings. By the end of class, he was smiling and having fun again and we were back on track.

Several weeks later, Max received his new belt. He was jumping for joy and screaming, "I did it! I did it!!" as he moved across the classroom floor. I walked with him over to his family, smiled and simply said,

"Aren't you glad you didn't quit that day. Because you never would have had the chance to feel this way and enjoy the success of your hard work."

How To Double Your Child's Self-Confidence in Just 30 Days

PAST SUCCESS BUILDS FUTURE CONFIDENCE

It is important to remind your child of past victories and accomplishments. I constantly hear everywhere I go, how negative people are and critical when they speak. It is so easy to be negative and find the things to pick on if you look for them.

 In fact, it has become second nature to most people. Almost gone are the days when our parents taught us, "If you don't have anything nice to say, don't say anything at all." It has become the, "You are going to hear what I think of you." It is really unfortunate, especially when you are dealing with children. Parents forget the impact they have and the words they choose matter! With children, you want to focus on two things.

First, children are present minded until at least the age of 12. What that means is, the only thing that exists to your child is what is right there in front of them right at that moment. They are not going to remember their past victories or how much they liked to do something in the past. Also, they are not able to picture things in the future.

I can use my martial arts school as a perfect example. If a child is sitting here playing with his best friend, or if they are playing their video game, or watching their favorite cartoon, and a parent comes in and says,

"Hey, come on. It is time to go to karate."

It does not matter how much fun that child has had in karate for the past couple of years. They are thinking,

"I don't want to go, I am watching this, or I am doing this." So you start getting resistance at that point. By being able to point to some of their past victories or their past accomplishments,

"Hey remember when you got that belt?"

20
How To Double Your Child's Self-Confidence in Just 30 Days

"Didn't you feel good reaching your goal?"
"Do you remember how you felt when ...?"

Being able to realize that kids are not able to draw on their past, and that their mentality is not yet developed to draw on those past experiences. Being the parent, that is part of your responsibility. Point those things out to your child and remind them of how they felt.

Second, the parent needs to become the "good finder." Again, it is easy to be critical. It is easy to point out the things that you do not like. Really think of your role as a parent, or mentor, or coach, whatever title you have with a child that you want to be the "good finder."

Instead of saying,

"These two things were nice but these four things were bad," you ignore the four bad things.
"Yeah, you did a great job on these two things."

A lot of times I will sit down with parents and they are just baffled when I speak with them.

Parent: *"Well my child is just acting so badly, A, B, C, D."*
They just give me the laundry list of terrible things.

Me: I will ask them, *"What is one good thing?"*

They will literally just stare at me. They cannot think of one. Here I am, I have known the child for maybe an hour, maybe a week and I can pick four or five good things right off the top of my head.

What I have learned is that looking for the positive in a situation is a skill. It is not anything that people just do. You have to practice this skill to make it better. And continue to practice it until it becomes natural.

ASSIGNMENT #3

Practice being the biggest cheerleader possible for your child. Look for the ONE thing they do well and celebrate it. Ignore all other things that you did not like. Ignore the temptation to correct or criticize. By celebrating the positive thing, your child will want to do more of those positive things and in time, they will eventually do the whole thing well.

For a video that will show you "good finder" examples and help you become a Black Belt Parent, visit http://DennyStrecker.com/confidencebook-bonus

There are lots of free examples are in the included as a bonus for buying my book.

CHAPTER 4. FOCUS ON IMPROVEMENT – NOT PERFECTION

"Have no fear of perfection - you'll never reach it."
- Salvador Dali

THE FOX AND THE GRAPES

One hot summer's day a Fox was strolling through an orchard till he came to a bunch of Grapes just ripening on a vine which had been trained over a lofty branch. "Just the thing to quench my thirst," quoth he. Drawing back a few paces, he took a run and a jump, and just missed the bunch.

Turning round again with a One, Two, Three, he jumped up, but with no greater success. Again and again he tried after the tempting morsel, but at last had to give it up, and walked away with his nose in the air, saying: "I am sure they are sour."

It is easy to despise what you cannot get.

SMALL THINGS MAKE A BIG DIFFERENCE

Now let's talk about focusing on improvement not perfection. There are a lot kids who get it in their head that if they cannot do something perfectly the first time, then they will not do it at all. That thinking is so limiting and will create such a struggle and problems for the child. What you want to do is focus on improvement - however small.. Your child might be misbehaving six days out of the seven. Instead of looking at those six days, look at the one day. Hey, there was improvement. They used to misbehave all seven days. By focusing on little improvements you can find the things that worked on that one day and try to repeat those skills or habits every day.

My next challenge for you is to remove the word "No" from your vocabulary. Boy does this get parents to raise their eyebrows. I am not telling you to

23

never tell your child "no." What I am asking is that you remove the word "no" from the sentence or your vocabulary all together. Here is an example.

A seventh grade girl came home and was very excited. She met a boy that was in high school. He asked her to go to the high school prom.

The parent is sitting here thinking oh my god, my seventh grade wants to go out with a high schooler and there is no way this is going to happen.

Naturally your knee jerk reaction is going to be, "Absolutely not!!" That ends all conversation between the child and the parent. So instead, you change that conversation. The mom says, *"Absolutely you can go, once you are in high school."*

Look at that sentence again. She said no but she did not have to use the word "no." With our negative culture and our negative society, this is a huge challenge for all parents. Go back to we are not looking for perfection but we are focusing on improvement. I am not saying okay by the time you are done reading this book, "no" is out of your vocabulary. What I am saying though is start tracking how many times you tell your child "no" and see about decreasing it. If you decrease it enough, eventually you are going to hit zero and you are going to have developed this new skill.

ASSIGNMENT #4

Start tracking the good things your child does by creating a Success Journal. Every time your child does something "good" write in the journal. Then, any time they are getting down on themselves, pull it out and have them read through the past accomplishments.

Part of this assignment is to see how many times a day you use the word "No" and find creative ways to still say it without using that word.

For a bonus report "100 Ways to Positively Reinforce Your Child", visit http://DennyStrecker.com/confidencebook-bonus

Lots of free examples are in the included as a bonus for buying my book.

How To Double Your Child's Self-Confidence in Just 30 Days

Chapter 5. Develop a Family Heritage

"Family is not an important thing. It's everything."
- Michael J. Fox

The Bundle of Sticks

A husbandman, who had a quarrelsome family, after having tried in vain to reconcile them by words, thought he might more readily prevail by an example. So he called his sons and bade them lay a bundle of sticks before him. Then having tied them into a faggot, he told the lads, one after the other, to take it up and break it. They all tried, but tried in vain.

Then untying the faggot, he gave them the sticks to break one by one. This they did with the greatest ease. Then said the father, "Thus you, my sons, as long as you remain united, are a match for all your enemies; but differ and separate, and you are undone."

What Things Does Your Family Do?

Developing a family heritage is something that has fallen by the wayside. Back in the day, it used to be a big thing for the entire family to go and find their Christmas tree and to cut it down and bring it back to the house. It is something that a small group of people still do today, but most families no longer do it.

Having something that the family does, is important. For example, do you remember those dreaded family vacations? It meant getting in the car and driving across the country to some supposedly "fun" place. You are going to do it because we are family. As much as we hated that trip, we spent time together which developed stories and a family history.

Find something that you can do as a family, and then build on it. It can be something simple like a monthly movie night at home, an afternoon at the park, or trip to get dessert somewhere.

ASSIGNMENT #5

Start to develop your family heritage by finding things to do as a family. Make a list of activities that each family member finds fun and then ask the other members if they would enjoy doing that activity too. The activities with the most votes go to the top of the list.

Start having a family meeting and allowing everyone to speak and tell you about their ideas and wants for the family. This is a great way to give everyone a chance to have a voice in what goes on and to understand what things are "coming up" so they are not surprised or resistant to it.

For a bonus report "100 Ways to Positively Reinforce Your Child", visit http://DennyStrecker.com/confidencebook-bonus

Lots of free examples are in the included as a bonus for buying my book.

Chapter 6. Provide Feedback in a Positive Loving Fashion

"We must return optimism to our parenting. To focus on the joys, not the hassles; the love, not the disappointments; the common sense, not the complexities." - **Fred G. Gosman**

Children Mimic What They See

I have seen this scenario too many times in my years of teaching. Maybe you have seen it too. Carl was 7 years old and was not the best student in my class. He did not have very much focus, he had a difficult time remembering tasks, his communication skills were poor and he lacked confidence about everything in his life.. Carl has been in my karate class for about a year before I ever saw mom watch a class. When she started watching class, it did not take long to figure out why Carl struggled so much with his confidence. I had started class with the usual warm up exercises and suddenly I hear,

"You call those push ups?"

I was rather surprised as parents know better than to talk to their child while in class. (It distracts them so they are not able to focus on what I am saying) A minute later,

"Come on, you are slowing the class down." Followed by,
"You really suck."

WHAT?!?! I could not believe that a parent would actually say that to their child let alone to them while they are standing in class!!

So it became instantly clear why Carl had zero confidence. He was beaten down verbally by the person who is supposed to be is biggest cheerleader.

Become the Good Finder For Your Child

Parents need to provide feedback in a positive loving fashion. Again, goes back to that it's easy to be critical, it is easy to be negative. The idea here is always try to be that nurturer which is a skill that needs to be learned. I am finding that parents either don't want to possess this skill, don't know about, or haven't even thought about it.

You are frustrated, your day has been rough, your boss has yelled at you, so there is a tendency for everything to roll downhill. So you end up snapping at your spouse, significant other or your kids.

One of the skills that I teach my martial arts students to prevent this from happening is, whatever attitude, negative or bad feelings you have, you leave them at the door. One of my students asked me, "Do you mean the karate door, or do you mean any door?" That was a great question. Why not leave it at any door. You had a bad day at work, you leave it at the door when you walk in your house.

Your house is supposed to be a domicile. It is supposed to be safe. It is the place that you are looking forward to getting to because it is safe. If you don't have that feeling then by all means you are going to have stress in your life, and it is going to add stress to the life of your children.
See what you need to do to change that, and make your home your sanctuary. You will find that your life is so incredibly better you will wonder how you ever did without it.

By being able to provide that feedback in a positive loving manner, instead of snapping or God forbid, using sarcasm when talking to your kids. Parents who do are then shocked when it comes back at them. I shake my head and say, "Well where do you think they learned it from?" The parent just stares at me with those blank eyes again. Sarcasm doesn't work. You want to be the nurturer. You want to make every experience a loving caring one. Positive feedback is best. Another goal would be to remove the word "but" from your vocabulary. Right after the word "no" remove the word "but."

What I teach is the word "But" is an interjection in the middle of a sentence that says here is what I am thinking <u>but</u> now here is my excuse why not. So an example would be,

"Hey, can you help me move some of my furniture this weekend?"

"I would love to." And everybody knows what is next.
"But I've got this to do instead."

It kills the conversation. People don't remember anything that was said before the word "but." They don't remember that you wanted to, or that you would like to help. They just remember that you were busy. Think about that, if you give your wife or girlfriend a compliment,

*"Hey, that is a really nice dress, **BUT** I don't like how it hangs on your hips."*

I can guarantee you she is not going to remember the fact that you said that you liked the dress.

Here is a fun challenge for you to do. Remove the word "but" from your vocabulary.

ASSIGNMENT #6

It is your responsibility as a parent to be your child's biggest fan. Positive feedback will go a long way to helping them want to learn and experience new things in their life. If they only experience negative feedback, they will tend to become shy and introverted and fearful of anything new. That is no way to live.

Now, I am not saying you can never be negative. I would suggest a solid 2 to 1 ratio. For every negative comment you make to your child, make sure you find 2 good ones some place else.

If you follow this simple formula, you will see your child bloom and grow and be happy to try new things and experiences.

Would you like to get free updates and some _COOL_ gifts?
I am constantly working on new skills and adding techniques to my toolkit. When I add something to this book, you will get it for free. Just visit:

http://DennyStrecker.com/25thingsbook

How To Double Your Child's Self-Confidence in Just 30 Days

CHAPTER 7. TEACH THE VALUE OF TELLING THE TRUTH

"Whoever is careless with the truth in small matters cannot be trusted with important matters." - **Albert Einstein**

THE WISE MASTER

There once was a teacher who lived with a great number of students in a run-down old school

The students supported themselves by begging for food in the bustling streets of a nearby town. Some of the students grumbled about their humble living conditions. In response, the old master said one day, "We must repair the walls of this temple. Since we occupy ourselves with study and meditation, there is no time to earn the money we will need. I have thought of a simple solution."

All the students eagerly gathered closer to hear the words of their teacher.

The master said, "Each of you must go into the town and steal goods that can be sold for money. In this way, we will be able to do the good work of repairing our temple."

The students were startled at this suggestion from their wise master. But since they respected him greatly, they assumed he must have good judgment and did not protest.

The wise master said sternly, "In order not to defile our excellent reputation by committing illegal and immoral acts, please be certain to steal when no one is looking. I do not want anyone to be caught."

When the teacher walked away, the students discussed the plan among themselves. "It is wrong to steal," said one. "Why has our wise master asked us to do this?"

Another retorted, "It will allow us to build our temple, which is a good result. " They all agreed that their teacher was wise and just and must have a sensible reason for making such an unusual request. They set out eagerly for the town, promising each other that they would not disgrace their school by getting caught. "Be careful," they called to one another. "Do not let anyone see you stealing. "

All the students except one young boy set forth. The wise master approached him and asked, "Why do you stay behind?"

The boy responded, "I cannot follow your instructions to steal where no one will see me. Wherever I go, I am always there watching. My own eyes will see me steal."

The wise master tearfully embraced the boy. "I was just testing the integrity of my students," he said. "You are the only one who has passed the test!"

The boy went on to become a great teacher himself.

WHITE LIES ARE STILL LIES

It is important for parents to teach the value of telling the truth. Hopefully, you already practice this habit. Little lies are still lies. There is no such thing as a ... Well there is such a thing as a "white lie", but it is still a lie. You can split the hairs all you want.

I did not lie, I just didn't tell you the truth - that is a lie.
I didn't lie, I just didn't say anything, that's a lie.

If you allow your child to split hairs like that, then you are setting yourself up for a whole list of problems down the road as they get older.

33
How To Double Your Child's Self-Confidence in Just 30 Days

Here is a true story about how some parents think. This is becoming so common it scares me to death. Hannah Montana is one of the Disney characters who was on Nickelodeon until 2011. The tv station held an essay contest and the winner would receive tickets to her concert. The center of the controversy was that the mother attached a note to the essay saying that the girl's father was in Iraq and was killed over there, so her daughter really needed these tickets to get through this traumatic event. It turned out, not only was dad not killed in Iraq, dad was not even a soldier in the military. When the truth came out, there was a major backlash towards the mom, as you can imagine.

I am shocked that she would go that far. Now the mom in all this aftermath was sitting there saying,

"Well I don't understand why everybody is so mad. I have had to take my "My Space" page off the internet because I am getting hate calls, or emails. People are calling my house. We had to move. I haven't been able to be at home."

She is shocked that people are that appalled that she lied. She didn't see it as a lie. When the story broke she literally told her daughter, "Well they *said* we lied so they didn't give us the tickets." So even to this day she is denying the fact that she lied. She doesn't see it as a lie.

What message is she teaching her child? That it is okay to lie, or to justify it in any fashion. So in turn, the child grows up and believes it is ok to lie.

This goes for everything. You take your kids to the movie and your child is 10 years old, and the child ticket is for 9 and under. You tell them, "Well tell them you are nine." That is a lie. You are teaching them at that moment that it is okay to lie.

Now on the flip side, what comes to mind is that you don't want to double punish your child when they do tell the truth. Here is a personal example of what I mean. When I was a youngster, our school class went on a field trip. I lived in Michigan and we took the train over to Toronto, and stayed in a

How To Double Your Child's Self-Confidence in Just 30 Days

hotel.

 This was elementary school, so a REALLY REALLY long time ago. What ended up happening is; we messed around and we did some things we should not have been doing. What exactly happened isn't critical. It wasn't anything major but we got in trouble. There were five or six of us in a room. The other four are the ones that got caught getting into trouble and they tried to lie about it. I was a little bit smarter and was able to hide a little bit better so I did not get into trouble at first. At the point the other four found out they were in trouble, I stepped forward and said that I was part of the group too. I was not innocent. I did this as well.

Well, I got punished just as everybody else who lied about doing anything the whole time. What did that lesson teach me?

It taught me that I might as well try to lie because if I get away with it then I am not going to get into trouble. If I get caught, I was going to be in trouble anyway.

My point is, if your child does tell the truth, you point that out, and you thank them for being honest. You let them know there is still a consequence because what they did was wrong, but because they told you the truth about it, it will not be as severe. So your child is being rewarded for telling the truth, but they are not off the hook for the thing they did. But never double punish your child for telling you the truth.

How To Double Your Child's Self-Confidence in Just 30 Days

ASSIGNMENT #7

Understanding why children lie will help you in the long run to deal with a wide variety of situations. Steering your child away from the desire to lie is an important step to their development. First and foremost, do your best to walk the talk. Show your child the importance of telling the truth by doing it yourself.

Look for opportunities to have conversations with your child about lying. Watch a television show, cartoon or movie and when you see someone lying, ask your child what they think about that. You may just be surprised at the answer you get.

Would you like to get free updates and some _COOL_ gifts?
I am constantly working on new skills and adding techniques to my toolkit.
When I add something to this book, you will get it for free. Just visit:

http://DennyStrecker.com/confidencebook-bonus

CHAPTER 8. TEACH YOUR CHILD TO TAKE PRIDE IN THEIR APPEARANCE

"Beauty is when you can appreciate yourself. When you love yourself, that's when you're most beautiful." - **Zoe Kravitz**

ZIG ZIGLAR ON APPEARANCE COUNTS

According to a study I read, the way we look has a direct bearing on our paycheck. Employment data from 7,000 adults was analyzed. Interviewers divided the group according to looks and then compared what those working similar jobs in each category were paid. Those who were below average in appearance earned less than those rated "average." Those who rated average earned less than those who were rated "above average."

Appearance includes many things. The style and neatness of your clothing, the shine on your shoes, the crease in your shirt, your choice of colors, and a host of other things affect your "appearance rating." The way you fix your hair, your make-up, and all the elements of your personal grooming make a contribution.

However, the biggest factor is the smile on your face, followed closely by your attitude and sense of humor. A good sense of humor and a positive attitude are particularly important as you move into the upper echelons of business. The reality is that people promote people. Evidence is solid that when everything else is equal, we will promote the person we like versus the one about whom we might feel either neutral or negative almost regardless of their skills.

The question is, who do we like? I believe you will agree that the people who are pleasant, cheerful and optimistic are easier to like than the ones who are inclined to be dour and even negative in their approach to life. It's also true that the cheerful, optimistic person is going to get more done and will have more cooperation from his or her fellow workers than will the negative individual. It is a practical matter that employers seek those who "fit," get more done, and are pleasant to be around.

So let your "Sunday best" appearance include a smile, a great attitude and an easy sense of humor. Try it and I'll bet you, too, will join the ranks of the "above average" in salary and success in life.

YOUR APPEARANCE MATTERS

Teach your child to take pride in their appearance. Again, for the sake of conversation, you see the kids these days walking around. Their hair is not cut. You just see the long shaggy hair. It's not combed. It's not groomed. The pants that hang halfway down so that you can see their underwear, and that is a fashion statement.

Ugh, I have yet to see the true essence of the fashion statement that way. Again, you have got some schools that require uniforms, ties, and suits. I don't think you need to go that far but teach your child to take pride. They should want to take a shower because nobody likes to be around somebody who smells.

Parents should give them some leeway about hair. It doesn't have to be the military haircut, straight at an inch and a half. You certainly want to have some freedom but take pride in exactly what that is, and at the same time set some standards. I hear parents negotiating with their kids about cutting their hair. If it is not acceptable the way it is then they have got to fix it. Tell them this is the way it is, period.

You can do whatever you want, but you have to be able to follow these guidelines. By teaching them to take pride in their appearance they are going to feel better about themselves in the long run. It is natural that if you go to church and you have got those Sunday clothes, everybody feels better when they are dressed up. You may not feel comfortable, but the idea is you look better, so you feel better.

How To Double Your Child's Self-Confidence in Just 30 Days

In the past I was what is called a "karate bum." I always wore sweatpants to school. When I got to school I changed into my karate uniform. That was comfortable. But what I found is people really didn't take me very seriously as an educator, or as a business person.

Once we started doing these different events, I went out and bought a nice suit, wore it to a family function a week later. Everybody was just in awe that I actually got dressed for the event. So that taught me right there that I should be taking pride in the way I look and the way I dress. It is that important.

Now granted you can always go to the far end too. You don't have to have the super expensive designer clothes on every single thing. That is not what I am saying. It is just a matter of taking the pride in looking your best with what you are also comfortable in wearing.

ASSIGNMENT #8

Teaching your child to take pride in their appearance and things is not something many parents think about very often. We all know that people like to make judgments without all the information, so if you look a certain way, you are very likely to be treated that way. So why not stack the deck in your child's favor by teaching to pay attention to how they look?

It is also a very important trait to learn so as they get older, they will take good care of their things. Children who don't care about their personal things tend to have trouble as they get older because their "things" become bigger and more expensive. What happens if you don't take care of your car or your house? Well, neglect it for too long and something major will cause either to break or fall apart.

Would you like to get free updates and some _COOL_ gifts?
I am constantly working on new skills and adding techniques to my toolkit. When I add something to this book, you will get it for free. Just visit:

http://DennyStrecker.com/confidencebook-bonus

CHAPTER 9. AVOID NEGATIVE PEOPLE

"You cannot have a positive life and a negative mind."
- Joyce Meyer

THE FOX WHO HAD LOST HIS TAIL

A FOX caught in a trap escaped, but in so doing lost his tail.
Thereafter, feeling his life a burden from the shame and ridicule to which he was exposed, he schemed to convince all the other Foxes that being tailless was much more attractive, thus making up for his own deprivation. He assembled a good many Foxes and publicly advised them to cut off their tails, saying that they would not only look much better without them, but that they would get rid of the weight of the brush, which was a very great inconvenience. One of them interrupting him and said, "If you had not yourself lost your tail, my friend, you would not thus
counsel us."

SOAR WITH THE EAGLES

Avoiding negative people is a big challenge since there are so many in the world. If you are around negative people all the time, it can bring your attitude down. It can make you negative. I use the example of the overweight women's bowling team. One of the ladies on the team decides,

"I want to feel better about myself, I'm going to look better. I'm going to lose some weight."

She starts to lose a couple of pounds. Do all of the other ladies on the bowling team say,

"Great job. You are doing awesome. You look so much better?"

How To Double Your Child's Self-Confidence in Just 30 Days

No. Usually what happens is, the women start to say things like,

"Why are you dieting?"
"You look good the way you are. You don't need to do that."

What tends to happen when you are trying to better yourself, everybody else starts to feel jealous, some consciously and others subconsciously. So what they do is they try to pull you back down with the group.

This is a great skill for adults to have also, and especially as a skill to pass on to your children. Anytime you try to set yourself apart, people are going to try to drag you down because they are jealous. Sometimes this jealousy is direct and immediate. Other times, it is a little sneakier. People tend to get comfortable with themselves and anything (or anyone) who comes along and disrupts that comfort is a problem. People do not like to feel uncomfortable, so they end up attacking the thing until it goes away.

For example: what do we say about the one kid in school who had all the answers to the teacher's questions?

"What a brown noser."

If you think back to that time in elementary school, yes we were jealous because someone else had the answers. Of course, being kids at the time we ended up making fun of the one who answered.

If you see that your child's friends are negative then it is time to step in and say,

"It's time to find some new friends."

Go back to those five skills I gave you for making friends, and start to use them to find a better set of friends.. That is one of the big ideas that I am trying to develop in my martial arts school. The sense of community. In the old days it took a village to raise a child, and in these days we don't want the village anywhere near our kids. It is a real shame and it is a real loss for everybody that this idea is fading in our culture.

What I do in the martial arts school is just that. We have one team and it is the martial arts team, and every student, and every parent, and ever sibling of a student in the school is part of the team. Everybody belongs, everybody plays, everybody gets along. You may not like somebody else on the team, but you are going to be respectful and get along.

It is always positive mindset that I stress to the children. When people walk in the door that is what I constantly hear,

"I really like coming to this school because I forget about everything else bad that has happened that day."

That is what I really focus on - make every visit a happy experience. The easiest way to do that is to avoid negative people that I call time vampires. People are going to sit and they are going to want to tell you what is going on in their life and how bad it is so that you feel sorry for them. Make it a point not to listen.

"Hey, I don't have time for this. I've got to go do my thing and be focused on the positive."

Start with yourself, and then spread it to your kids. It will be pleasantly surprised how much better your home begins to feel and how much more you want to be there.

ASSIGNMENT #9

Teaching your child how to avoid negative people in their life will save them decades of grief. Nothing is worse than getting sucked into someone else's vortex of "poor me" stories that have no solution because the person does not want one. Believe it or not, some people only seem to be happy when they are miserable. How crazy is that?

The old adage that misery loves company is absolutely true. It takes work to cut out and avoid such negativity but I absolutely guarantee you that once you do, you will enjoy your life a whole lot more.

Would you like to get free updates and some _COOL_ gifts?
I am constantly working on new skills and adding techniques to my toolkit.
When I add something to this book, you will get it for free. Just visit:

http://DennyStrecker.com/confidencebook-bonus

CHAPTER 10. PAINT A BIG PICTURE

"All successful people men and women are big dreamers. They imagine what their future could be, ideal in every respect, and then they work every day toward their distant vision, that goal or purpose." **- Brian Tracy**

THE ANT AND THE COCOON

An Ant nimbly running about in the sunshine in search of food came across a Cocoon that was very near its time of change. The Cocoon moved its tail, and thus attracted the attention of the Ant, who then saw for the first time that it was alive. "Poor, pitiable animal!" cried the Ant disdainfully. "What a sad fate is yours! While I can run hither and thither, at my pleasure, and, if I wish, ascend the tallest tree, you lie imprisoned here in your shell, with power only to move a joint or two of your scaly tail." The Cocoon heard all this, but did not try to make any reply.

A few days after, when the Ant passed that way again, nothing but the shell remained. Wondering what had become of its contents, he felt himself suddenly shaded and fanned by the gorgeous wings of a beautiful Butterfly. "Behold in me," said the Butterfly, "your much-pitied friend! Boast now of your powers to run and climb as long as you can get me to listen." So saying, the Butterfly rose in the air, and, borne along and aloft on the summer breeze, was soon lost to the sight of the Ant forever.

THE BIG PICTURE

It is amazing to me working with kids day in and day out, that they don't have any goal setting skills. Thinking back all the way to Chapter One, it is because parents just expect it.

Think about it: have you honestly ever sat down and taught your child how to set a goal? Not only do that, but how to check up on it and how to adjust it.

How To Double Your Child's Self-Confidence in Just 30 Days

Then once the goal is accomplished, how to set another one?

What I have started to do with all of the kids that I work with now is to say to them,

"You always have to have five goals that you are actively working on and they have to be written down."

That is one of the five aspects of a goal. It has to be written down. This step alone has really got the kids starting to think. Of course, the first several months you do this with your child, it is going to be really basic and sloppy. But again, we are not looking for perfection, we are moving towards improvement. So I encourage you to do this with your kids. Ask them,

"What is it you want?"
"Well I want to earn an A in this class."
"Okay, well what do you have to do to do that?"
"Well I've got to get A's on my quizzes."
"When are your quizzes?"
"Okay, so you're going to study here, and here, and here."
Actually sit down and do this with them. Take them through the process step by step, over, and over, and over again until they can show you they can do it without your help.

Then you know what you do? You check on them anyway.

Check in and follow up every so often with them. You kind of check in, "Hey great, yep still going." It is a matter of managing what it is you expect now that you have taught this habit. This is one of Steven Covey's "Seven Habits of Highly of Effective People".

Your second task in this chapter is to create a journal. I am surprised with the lack of writing skills kids have these days. I started giving the kids some brain teasers that they could write out. I literally watched kids take over 30 minutes to write four short sentences. This just shocked me. We are expecting writing skills but it does not appear to being taught. So let's put something in place that is going to help them with that.

Creating a journal I found has done that. By just writing in what your child is expected to do tomorrow, next week, in another month, or what did they do today, what did they accomplish. This is also going to allow you to thumb through the journal in six months and say,

"Hey you remember that. Wasn't that neat."

It is going to give you that information to go back to those good times and remember those victories. What I love about this process this that it is not limited to kids.

If you do not have a journal that you are writing in, get started on one. Use it when you are feeling down so you have something to look back at to remember that you are a good parent.

I get phone calls or emails saying, "I'm the worst parent in the world. I just suck as a parent. I'm doing everything wrong." The trigger was usually your significant other or spouse just beat you up over something that you did or didn't do, or the kids are sitting there in your face telling you, "I hate you." Look in your journal and find your victories.

I have sat down with many mothers and watched the heartbreak in their eyes as they are being told from their child that, *"I hate you."* If you have got your journal, those are the times that you can really dig, look back and reaffirm "Hey I am not, and I'm not a bad parent."

You can read and remember, *"I have done these things."*
It can beat that negative cycle.

Your final step would be if there is something that is a large goal, make sure you break it down into smaller steps. So take a little time and instead of trying to chunk one huge thing, "Hey, I've got this book report and it is due in

47

three weeks, okay go." Break it up into little things.

When are you going to have the reading part of it done? When you going to have the research done?
When are you going to have the outline done?

If you need to break it down smaller than that, do it.
It doesn't matter how many steps it takes to success.
It is a matter that you have to take those steps.

One of the greatest skills a parent has got to have (as I'm sure everybody knows that is reading this book) is patience. Once you lose your patience then all learning stops. As soon as you get angry and you start lecturing, or you start yelling, all learning has stopped. So that is another bonus for you here. Even under extreme circumstances, you should try to never yell at your kids. Think about when we were kids. As soon as my mom started yelling, click. I would turn right off thinking,

"Yep, here she goes again. She is going to rant for about three or four minutes and then I can be about my way."

So make it a goal to not lose your cool and to be able to be patient with them, and treat this as a good learning experience for them. Of course, there are those times where all else has failed and you may just lose your cool. That is ok too. Just do your best to make it the exception and and not the general rule.

ASSIGNMENT #10

Being able to see the Big Picture will help your child in a variety of ways as they grow up. Being to set goals and know how to achieve them will give them a major advantage of the majority of children their age. Most kids float through life. Help your child build a path to where they want to go and they will get to places they never dreamed they could. But you have to have a plan in place or they will never reach their full potential.

Would you like to get free updates and some _COOL_ gifts?
I am constantly working on new skills and adding techniques to my toolkit. When I add something to this book, you will get it for free. Just visit:

http://DennyStrecker.com/confidencebook-bonus

CHAPTER 11. RULES AND CONSEQUENCES

"You gain strength, courage, and confidence by every experience in which you really stop to look fear in the face. You are able to say to yourself, 'I lived through this horror. I can take the next thing that comes along."
- Eleanor Roosevelt

THE FOX AND THE GOAT

A Fox one day fell into a deep well and could find no means of escape. A Goat, overcome with thirst, came to the same well, and seeing the Fox, inquired if the water was good. Concealing his sad plight under a merry guise, the Fox indulged in a lavish praise of the water, saying it was excellent beyond measure, and encouraging him to descend. The Goat, mindful only of his thirst, thoughtlessly jumped down, but just as he drank, the Fox informed him of the difficulty they were both in and suggested a scheme for their common escape. "If," said he, "you will place your forefeet upon the wall and bend your head, I will run up your back and escape, and will help you out afterwards." The Goat readily assented and the Fox leaped upon his back. Steadying himself with the Goat's horns, he safely reached the mouth of the well and made off as fast as he could. When the Goat upbraided him for breaking his promise, he turned around and cried out, "You foolish old fellow! If you had as many brains in your head as you have hairs in your beard, you would never have gone down before you had inspected the way up, nor have exposed yourself to dangers from which you had no means of escape.

How To Double Your Child's Self-Confidence in Just 30 Days

CHILDREN LIKE RULES AND STRUCTURE...WHAT?

Rules and consequences come into play quite a bit from the standpoint that parents have got to set boundaries for the kids. Rules generally aren't too much of a problem for parents. On occasion, there is one parent that doesn't really like to have rules or enforce them. Then, the other parent is forced to play the bad cop all the time. This is a topic for another time.

The biggest thing that you have to make sure of is that consequences for bad behavior are in place. Whenever I talk to parents about an issue or a challenge that they are having, that is pretty much what I find the majority of the time. There are not consequences and the parent is frustrated trying to figure out why the rule isn't working. It is pretty straightforward, it is because there are no consequences. My father always says,

"If there are no consequences for bad behavior, bad behavior will continue."

Some of the guidelines to know are:

#1 - the consequence has to be clear
#2 - it has to be understood by the child
#3 - it has to be known prior to the rule being broken.

Otherwise, it is just punishment and anytime that you are just punishing your child, that is not necessarily fair. Here is an example for you:

Your boss walks up to your desk and says,

"Hey, you forgot to do this. I'm going to dock you one week's pay,"
You say, *"Well, you never told me to do that."*
"Well, it doesn't matter, you're supposed to know."

You would feel pretty upset, right? Well, a lot of times, that is how parents approach raising their children and it is that same process that it is really not very fair You want to make sure that there are clear consequences in place. In short, if you do A, B is going to happen.

I have worked a lot with parents (it seems like spring fever sets in and the kids are test the waters and act more.) One example would be,

"My child kept touching another child at school. The teacher told him to stop it, he looked right at the teacher and then, he touched the other child again. He knew he wasn't supposed to be doing it, he knew that he was going to get in trouble for it but he just didn't care."

When I asked the parent right there,

"Okay, so what happened?"
The parent said, *"Well, what do you mean? He got in trouble."*
"Okay. Well, what happened?"
"Well, he got put on yellow."

They have a color coding system at this particular school and so what I said was,

"Okay, well there wasn't any real consequence to his behavior."

He broke a rule so it should be,

"Johnny, if you touch anyone again, then you are going to have to sit out of recess and you won't be able to go outside or you won't be able to play."

At that point, you have got a clear consequence and now the child can make the decision on how he or she is going to behave.

Here is a common mistake parent's make. They try to control the person and that never works. Again, apply it back to yourself in your work environment.

Anytime somebody tries to control you, your natural reaction is to rebel. Well, kids are no different.

Instead of trying to control the person, you always want to stop the bad behavior or get the child to the positive behavior that you want. That is why you say something like,

"If you do this again, this is what is going to happen."

By saying that, you are allowing the child to make a decision on what their next behavior is going to be; they get to make the choice. Change the behavior and all will be well. Don't change the behavior and receive the consequence.

The child knows exactly what is going to happen one way or the other. If they don't do it again, well that is the rule and we are going to be able to move forward and do fun things. If they choose to do it again, then you have got to make sure that there is a consequence in place. Right next to consequences to finish up this topic is also consistency.

I hear from parents all the time,

"Well, I even put the rules in place but my spouse doesn't follow along or they don't agree with them or they don't back me."

That is a tough situation. There is no simple answer to this issue. You have to either figure out a plan that works for your family, or ask your spouse to not interfere.

Let's continue on with the idea of consistency. If you are not consistent, then the kids are not going to know if the rules apply or not. A good example of this when the kids run up and say,

How To Double Your Child's Self-Confidence in Just 30 Days

"Mom. Mom. Mom. Mom. Mom. Mom. Mom. Mom," and they just go on and on. Finally after about the 12th time, the parent finally says, *"What?!"* and then listens to the child and answers them.

Instead, you should stop the situation. You look at your child and you say,

"I'm talking to somebody. You are being rude. You need to wait until I am done and then I will be happy to give you my full attention."

This teaches them patience and respect.

Another point that I generally add is that when a child approaches, they should raise their hand to speak to you instead of just talking over and over and over again.

The same thing goes with the word "no." If your child asks you to do something and you say "no."

Again, I see this day after day and it kills me.

"Mom, can I have this?"
"No."
"Can I have it please?"
"No."
"Can I have it please?"
"No."
"Can I have it please please please?"
"Well, okay here."

What you have just taught your child is this,

If mom says no, it doesn't mean no. If I ask five times, I am going to be able to get to a yes.

What I always try to put in place is elevated consequences.
I have absolutely no problem with a child asking for something. That is part of life and that is growing up and that is what we want, that communication.

"Mom, can I have this?"
"No."
"Mom, can I have this?"
"Okay, I said no once and if you ask me again, you are going to have to go to bed 10 minutes early tonight."

However you want to set it up. At that point, what you have done is you have elevated their risk so again, you are controlling the behavior, not the person.

They have to make a decision about how badly do they really want whatever it is. If they know if they ask again, the answer is going to be no and there is going to be a penalty attached to it, they are less likely to ask again.

It has never happened that I have had to go to the next stage and offer another penalty because as soon as I institute the first one, they see that I mean business and that I am serious and that pretty much takes care of the whole issue.

Now doing this once, is it going to take care of everything? Absolutely not. That is another thing that I hear a lot from parents,

"My child is 12 years old, they should be able to clean their room."

Right away, you are going to hear back from me,

"Well, only if you have taught them that particular skill."

Just because a child is however many years old, it doesn't automatically equate to being able to have a particular skill. We have got to teach them a skill just like right now. I am teaching you a parenting skill and it doesn't

55

matter if you are a 25-year-old parent, or a 50-year-old parent or even a grandparent. These skills are still going to apply but I don't expect you to know them until I have taught them to you.

Are you one of those parents that say,

"We don't have rules for our kids. They are self-guided."

That is not being a parent. Part of the responsibility of a parent is to set up boundaries and anybody that tells you that their child does better without rules is delusional. I will say that to their face, I will say it to your face, I will say it publicly, and I will say it privately.

<u>If you do not have rules and boundaries for kids, then you are headed down a path of serious trouble for a long, long time.</u>

ASSIGNMENT #11

Create a list of bad behaviors and then add a consequence next to each one. Go over this list with your child and post it on the refrigerator. Any time your child behaves badly, go to the list, remind them of the consequence and enforce it. This will eliminate most of the whining and complaining because the child knows about the list and you are just enforcing it.

Would you like to get free updates and some _COOL_ gifts?
I am constantly working on new skills and adding techniques to my toolkit. When I add something to this book, you will get it for free. Just visit:

http://DennyStrecker.com/confidencebook-bonus

How To Double Your Child's Self-Confidence in Just 30 Days

Chapter 12. Your Child Needs Your Time

"My favorite things in life don't cost any money. It's really clear that the most precious resource we all have is time."

- Steve Jobs

The Dog And The Wolf

A gaunt Wolf was almost dead with hunger when he happened to meet a House-dog who was passing by. "Ah, Cousin," said the Dog.

"I knew how it would be; your irregular life will soon be the ruin of you. Why do you not work steadily as I do, and get your food regularly given to you?"

"I would have no objection," said the Wolf, "if I could only get a place."

"I will easily arrange that for you," said the Dog; "come with me to my master and you shall share my work."

So the Wolf and the Dog went towards the town together. On the way there the Wolf noticed that the hair on a certain part of the Dog's neck was very much worn away, so he asked him how that had come about.

"Oh, it is nothing," said the Dog. "That is only the place where the collar is put on at night to keep me chained up; it chafes a bit, but one soon gets used to it."

"Is that all?" said the Wolf. "Then good-bye to you, Master Dog."

QUALITY TIME IS CRUCIAL

There are three different areas of quality time that need to be considered. The first and foremost is family time. "Quality" is the key word - Quality time. Time is a tough commodity for a lot of people. It is one of the key things that I work on with the kids in my program. I speak to my classes about Time Management just about every week. Being able to manage your time so that you are able to get more done within the set workday or the week, or whatever the length of time might be.

You probably know someone who is just notoriously late for everything that they do. I see it at my school too. If I have a class at 6:00, there are some parents walking in at five or 10 after. Then, if I move the class at 6:30, well they are still walking in five or 10 minutes late. They have not learned how to manage their time well.

To have quality time for your family, don't think of it as, *"We have got to set out a whole afternoon for this to work."*

Instead, it can be as simple as:

"Hey, every 10 minutes before bedtime, we are going to sit down and read a book," if reading is what your child likes to do or if that is what you like to do with your child.

It could be watch a family TV show, it could be go for a walk, any particular event as long as the quality part of that equation is making sure that your child has 100% of your attention. You don't take your cellphone, you don't have any other distractions, you turn the phone off if you have to in the house, put down your iPhone if you are into technology. Facebook will not disappear if you stop posting for an hour. Candy Crush or any other time vampire game will be fine if you don't play it for a while.

The world isn't going to end if you disconnect or unplug for 15 or 30 minutes a night to spend time with your family. Making sure that you get that quality time for the entire family is number one.

Number two, another thing that I see lacking in a lot of the situations with families is "parent" time. Parents have to have quality time too. You have to have that time with your spouse, just you and them, to be able to do things together. Not with the kids, not with other couples, just quality time for the two of you so that you can continue to enjoy your relationship.

This is key because these are some of the examples for your child. Being a parent, you are the ultimate role model. If you never go out with your spouse, or do something together, then your kids aren't going to see that relationship. What starts to happen, especially if it is an only child situation; the child starts to think the world revolves around them because everything you do involves them and your spouse does the same thing. That is not healthy for your child. They need to see the two of you interacting and enjoying each other.

If you are a single parent, this same rule applies. Obviously, instead of having "significant other" time, you are going to have your "alone" time.

"Hey, Mom's going out tonight,"
or if you are a father,
"Dad is going out tonight."

Showing the kids that you do have a life outside of them so that they start to see what is expected as you get a little bit older.

Number three is "Alone" time. Even if you are in a nuclear family situation with a spouse and maybe even an extended family with grandparents, each parent should take their alone time.

In some cases, mom doesn't have a job outside of the home and is at home

60
How To Double Your Child's Self-Confidence in Just 30 Days

with the kids all day. Dad comes home and he is tired and doesn't want to really spend too much time with the kids. He wants to watch TV or something. That starts to wear pretty thin very quickly. Mom deserves a break and some "alone" time, if she wants.

Each parent needs to have their activity or their thing to do that they can basically just get out of the house. Even if it is, an hour, a half hour, a half day, a full day. Do something that you enjoy doing and take a break and be able to come back more well balanced and ready to be part of the family.

ASSIGNMENT #12

A happy life is all about balance. When you are out of balance, you feel stress and unhappiness. Take a look at your routines - work, home, family, and self. Are all four of these in balance with each other? Most of the time, the answer is going to be, "No." At least _ONE_ of these are going to be out of balance and require more attention. The point is to get as close as you can to perfect balance. That means making sure to spend quality time with your children. It does not have to be a huge vacation or expensive event. The fact that you are making memories with them is the most important.

Create a list of quality time events that you would like to do with your children, ask them what things they think should be on the list, and then pull out your calendar and as best as you can, schedule them.

Would you like to get free updates and some _COOL_ gifts?
I am constantly working on new skills and adding techniques to my toolkit.
When I add something to this book, you will get it for free. Just visit:

http://DennyStrecker.com/confidencebook-bonus

CHAPTER 13. FAMILY MEETING

"Family is not an important thing. It's everything."
- Michael J. Fox

THE TWO DOGS

A man had two Dogs: a Hound, trained to assist him in his sports, and a House dog, taught to watch the house. When he returned home after a good day's sport, he always gave the House dog a large share of his spoil. The Hound, feeling much aggrieved at this, reproached his companion, saying, "It is very hard to have all this labor, while you, who do not assist in the chase, luxuriate on the fruits of my exertions." The House dog replied, "Do not blame me, my friend, but find fault with the master, who has not taught me to labor, but to depend for subsistence on the labor of others.

THE FAMILY MEETING

This is one thing that I don't see at all but that every family should be doing on a weekly basis. You should have a weekly family meeting.

By having this weekly meeting, you are teaching your children that they are part a group or team. We go through things together, we watch each other's back, we support each other, we want to know what is going on in each other's lives. This meeting will start to change or evolve over time depending on the age of the kids. If you have a toddler, they can, and should, still be involved in the meeting, but their input isn't going to be as significant as it might be if you have a teenager.

Here is how the meeting works. You sit down and ask,

"What's going on in this upcoming week? This is what we have scheduled. This is what we have planned. This is what we are doing, and here are some things

How To Double Your Child's Self-Confidence in Just 30 Days

that we would like to do."

Lay out your calendar of events. Start showing your children this time management skill and they will benefit from it for a lifetime. In a lot cases, this may be the first time the parents have used this skill too. What a great experience for the entire family to share.

This can be tough for some parents and that is ok. I am asked pretty often,

"How do I teach my child self-confidence if I don't have self-confidence?"

The answer is you can't. All of these skills that we are working on, you need to work on yourself first and then, be able to pass them on to your children by demonstration and role modeling.

With your family meetings, you are going to work on your time management, you are going to lay out your schedule, be able to talk about vacations;

"Hey, what are we going to do?
Where you guys want to go this summer?
What is one thing you would like to do this Saturday?
Hey, we have got to clean the garage. When are we going to do that?
Who is going to take care of the backyard and the mowing or the snow removal?"

It is not so much exactly what is said but it is important that everybody is at the table and everybody contributes to the conversation.

You are learning to work as a family unit and to be able to spend more quality time together and keep in touch with what is going on in everybody's life.

ASSIGNMENT #13

Hosting a Family Meeting is a big deal and goes a long way to making everyone in the family feel as though they are a part of it. Follow the steps described above and get your meeting in place as soon as possible. You will be happy that you did.

Would you like to get free updates and some _COOL_ gifts?
I am constantly working on new skills and adding techniques to my toolkit.
When I add something to this book, you will get it for free. Just visit:

http://DennyStrecker.com/confidencebook-bonus

How To Double Your Child's Self-Confidence in Just 30 Days

Chapter 14. Teach Respect

"I'm not concerned with your liking or disliking me...
All I ask is that you respect me as a human being."
- Jackie Robinson

The Lioness

A controversy prevailed among the beasts of the field as to which of the animals deserved the most credit for producing the greatest number of whelps at a birth. They rushed clamorously into the presence of the Lioness and demanded of her the settlement of the dispute.

"And you," they said, "how many sons have you at a birth?' The Lioness laughed at them, and said:

"Why! I have only one; but that one is altogether a thoroughbred Lion."

Be The Role Model of Respect.

One of my goals with this book is to spread the word to as many households as possible that, the number one rule in this household is,

"No yelling in the house, period. We don't raise our voices, we don't yell and scream. We talk like people and we talk with respect. If you are yelling and screaming, then all respect has gone out the window. Parents tend to yell at their kids. While there is a time and place that raising your voice can be effective, too many parents use it as their first form of discipline. No yelling in the house means just that - no yelling in the house. It is not no yelling in the house for the kids.

Remember, you have to role model and use the skill that you want your children to learn. You can take it to the point of extreme in this case too.

Let's say you are downstairs and the kids are upstairs and you scream upstairs for them, "Hey, it's dinnertime!" That is yelling in the house, and that is not acceptable. You walk up the stairs, you go get the kids or have one child go get another child if you have multiple kids in the family and vice versa. If your kids want to talk to you, they should not be yelling down the stairs or yelling from another room.

Another way that you can apply this rule is, if you are talking to me, then you need to have eye contact with me and make sure I have it with you. That way I know you are talking to me. Too often, a young student will come to class and be super excited to tell me something that they did that day. They will just jump right into their story without getting my attention. Then a couple of things can happen, either I did not hear the story because I was focused on something else, or they get their feelings hurt because they see I am not paying attention. Get eye contact first, and then I would love to hear your story.

Parents forget about this a lot of times. It is not going to automatically click. It is going to take some conscious effort and it is going to take work on your part.

When you start to teach respect, just think about the ways that you like to be treated. Look at the way you are treating others and the things that you say to people. For example, somebody cuts you off on the road and you swear or you let some words go that you shouldn't. Well, that is teaching your child. Read the poem, "Children learn what they live."
available on the bonus website I created for you. If they see you doing that, then they are going to think that it is the way that you deal with things - yell and scream when something doesn't go the right way for you.

ASSIGNMENT #14

Think of what respect means to you and what it looks like. Then set out to be the best role model of that behavior that you can be. You will be surprised at how quickly your children notice **AND** begin to mimic your behavior.

Would you like to get free updates and some _COOL_ gifts?
I am constantly working on new skills and adding techniques to my toolkit. When I add something to this book, you will get it for free. Just visit:

http://DennyStrecker.com/confidencebook-bonus

Chapter 15. Learn Something New

"Tell me and I forget.
Teach me and I remember.
Involve me and I learn."
- Benjamin Franklin

The Widow And The Sheep

A certain poor widow had one solitary Sheep. At shearing time, wishing to take his fleece and to avoid expense, she sheared him herself, but used the shears so unskillfully that with the fleece she sheared the flesh. The Sheep, writhing with pain, said, "Why do you hurt me so, Mistress? What weight can my blood add to the wool? If you want my flesh, there is the butcher, who will kill me in an instant; but if you want my fleece and wool, there is the shearer, who will shear and not hurt me.

Have Your Child Teach You

A great way to spend some of that quality time (from the previous chapter) is to have them teach you a particular activity. This is absolutely huge for their self-confidence. Getting them to the point where they know something that you don't and they are able to share that knowledge is going to make them feel great about themselves.

Their self-confidence and their self-esteem is going to skyrocket at that point. Does everything they show you have to be absolutely 100% correct? No, it never does. The idea is you just have them teaching it to you.

If you want it to be the latest video game, you say to your child,

"Teach me how to play this game or how to get to this level."

Or,

"Hey, what were you doing in school this week?"
"We worked on adding and subtracting."
"Well, great. It's been a long time since I have done that.
I was not very good at math in school.
Can you teach me?"

Have them teach you and then, at that point, you are say,

"Hey. Wow, that was great. I forgot all about that one point. You showed me something new, thank you very much."

Again, it does not matter what the activity is, but having your child teach you how to do it is going to give them that huge boost in self-confidence.

ASSIGNMENT #15

Make it a point to learn something that you are interested in and would like to know more about. Maybe it is woodcarving, or model building, or insects, or a language. It does not matter what it is, as long as you find it interesting.

Then, learn as much as you can about it and enjoy the process.

Would you like to get free updates and some _COOL_ gifts?
I am constantly working on new skills and adding techniques to my toolkit.
When I add something to this book, you will get it for free. Just visit:

http://DennyStrecker.com/confidencebook-bonus

How To Double Your Child's Self-Confidence in Just 30 Days

CHAPTER 16. THINKING POSITIVE

"In order to carry a positive action
we must develop here a positive vision."
- Dalai Lama

THE HUNTER AND THE WOODMAN

A hunter, not very bold, was searching for the tracks of a Lion. He asked a man felling oaks in the forest if he had seen any marks of his footsteps or knew where his lair was. "I will," said the man, "at once show you the Lion himself." The Hunter, turning very pale and chattering with his teeth from fear, replied, "No, thank you. I did not ask that; it is his track only I am in search of, not the Lion himself.

THINKING POSITIVE

One of the challenges that I give parents who have children in my program is, to remove negative words from their vocabulary. One of the things we talk about specifically is removing the word "no" from your vocabulary. Now, to be clear, I am not telling you to never tell your child "no." We are going to say "no" to them all the time because we have got rules and consequences in place. Success comes in how to say "no" without using the word "no."

For example, I had a seven-year-old come up to me while his mom stood behind him. She surprised me with this meeting because she did not let me know anything about the issue ahead of time. I guess the child wanted to quit karate and it was just about time for class to start and so what I am guessing happened is,

Child: *"I don't want to go, I want quit."*

How To Double Your Child's Self-Confidence in Just 30 Days

Mom: *"Okay, Mom says go talk to Shihan,"* (which is my title, master teacher) and she says, *"Well, go talk to Shihan and if he says okay, then we will quit."*

She could say that because she knows I am never going to say,

"Well, yeah. Okay, fine. You can quit."

The child comes up to me, and says,

"Shihan. I want to quit karate,"
I say, *"Sure, you can quit once you earn your Black Belt."*
He says, *"Okay, great."*

At this point, he turns around, walks away and starts to get his shoes and thinks he is done. Now, granted because he was not listening very clearly and he is used to just being told yes or no, he did not understand. Kids are used to hearing the word "no" all the time, that is why they ask five or six times to see if they can get through it.

Changing the conversation with him, I did two things. I was able to teach the parent how to say "no" without saying "no" and, at the same time, I was able to stop the student,

"Did you hear what I said?"
"Yeah, you said I could quit."
"That's not what I said. I said you could quit when you earned your Black Belt. What belt are you in right now?" *"Well, I'm a Blue Belt,"*
"Okay. Well, then you have got several more belts. Go get out on the floor."

He looked at me for a second, took off his shoes, went out on the floor and had a great class.

One of the important things to understand is that children are present-minded until around the age of twelve years old. This explains a common

73
How To Double Your Child's Self-Confidence in Just 30 Days

complaint I hear from parents,

"Well, my kid doesn't want to come to karate class but once they're here, they have a great time."

Well, absolutely. I can tell you exactly what is happening. They are either playing with their friends, playing their favorite video game or watching a cartoon and the parent comes in and says,

"Okay, it's time to go to karate. Let's go."

No matter how much fun your child has at karate that does not matter. They do not remember all of the fun times. They are sitting there doing their favorite thing right now, they do not want to leave it.

By using this skill and knowing that that kids are present-minded, they are only thinking about that one thing they are doing right at that moment. By being two or three steps ahead of them, you are able to guide them to the decision in a process that you want. Have the kids do something that they do not enjoy doing before any activity that they do enjoy. Then, when you say it is time to do the next thing, they will be excited to do it.

Getting back into thinking positively, and being able to remove negative words. The first step to creating any habit is to catch yourself using negative words and being able to replace them.

A classic example I use is when people say, "I have to."
"Well, how come you don't want to play, Daddy?"
"Well, because I have to go to work."

Again, subconsciously, what you are doing now is you are teaching your kids that work is bad because you HAVE to do it. Work is not bad. Work pays the bills. It is not that I HAVE to go to work, it is I GET to go to work.

*"Well, I **GET** to go to work because that is what gives us this nice house, give us food on the table and allows us to spend our quality time together."*

Now, this is a big challenge because a lot of people hate their job. If you fall into that category, then there are other issues that you need to address.

I am not condoning that you start lying to your child and you say how great work is, but at the same time, they don't need to know that your boss or manager is the worst manager in the world or whatever other adjectives you use to describe your work. That is not their business. Just being grateful that you have a job and that you have something that brings in money is all the kids need to know at this point. Then, as they get older, you can teach them the other things about work.

If you find yourself in a situation that you are not sure how to spin it and get out of removing the word "no" or how to change it to a positive sentence, by all means, send me an e-mail. I love those little challenges and like to see what we can put together for your specific situation.

How To Double Your Child's Self-Confidence in Just 30 Days

ASSIGNMENT #16

Are you a positive person? Do you think and speak in a positive way? You have to learn how to if you want your child to do it. This ties back into role modeling the behavior you want to see. Keep track of what you say and how you act for a couple of days and see if you tend to lean towards the negative or the positive.

If you lean towards the negative, you have got to change your thinking so you can change your language.

Would you like to get free updates and some _COOL_ gifts?
I am constantly working on new skills and adding techniques to my toolkit.
When I add something to this book, you will get it for free. Just visit:

http://DennyStrecker.com/confidencebook-bonus

CHAPTER 17. TEACH THE VALUE MONEY

"Money won't create success,
the freedom to make it will."
- Nelson Mandela

THE TWO FROGS

Two Frogs were neighbors. One inhabited a deep pond, far removed from public view; the other lived in a gully containing little water, and traversed by a country road. The Frog that lived in the pond warned his friend to change his residence and entreated him to come and live with him, saying that he would enjoy greater safety from danger and more abundant food. The other refused, saying that he felt it so very hard to leave a place to which he had become accustomed. A few days afterwards a heavy wagon passed through the gully and crushed him to death under its wheels.

TEACH THE VALUE OF MONEY

It can be tough to teach the value of money sometimes because some adults struggle with the concept themselves. They live on credit cards, and in way too much debt. They are working as much as they possibly can to try and reduce their debt, but end up just spinning their wheels. Or worse, get farther and farther behind no matter how hard they try.

If you are someone who has a lot of debt, you can still teach the value of money to your child. Are you role modeling a particular lifestyle that you cannot afford? If so, they are going to be inclined to pick up that bad habit. There is a big difference between being in debt and working your way out of it, and being in debt and wallowing in it. Working your way out will teach your child good habits. Wallowing will not.

Everybody's situation is different and so there are a lot of things we could discuss and work on here. For a basic start, do you give your child an allowance? This would be one place to start. I am not condoning if you do or if you don't, that is certainly a specific family choice. If you do give an allowance, what I would recommend is right off the top, you start taking 10% or 15% and teaching your kids about taxes. You write it out just like you see on your paychecks. You have got your federal withholding, your state withholding, sometimes you have city withholding and you have Social Security.

Now, the more important fact is what you do with that money. What I recommend is set that money aside. You put it into a separate account without telling the kids. Then, whatever landmark in their life comes along, maybe their 18th birthday or whatever situation you want. You give them that money back,

"Here is all the money that we took as taxes from your allowance growing up."

At that point, "Hey, they are going to buy a car. They are going to buy this or that big item." Then you can certainly help them out by giving them that extra cash.

Certainly teaching them that you don't get 100% of what you earned is going to be an important aspect. Another skill to develop is to be able to compare money to time. Everything in this world either costs you money or time.

It doesn't get any simpler than that. One of the things that I was looking at several years ago was having my house painted. Well, I had two choices:

#1 - I can either do it myself and it is going to take me two to three weeks to do it over multiple days and weekends

Or

#2 - I can pay somebody to come in and do it and they are going to be done

How To Double Your Child's Self-Confidence in Just 30 Days

in one or two days.

I have to invest my time or my money. So there is not a right or a wrong answer. It is up to me to decide which is more valuable.

Another concept parents can teach their child is how to barter.

"Hey, you want this item or this toy? Okay. Well, then you have to do this chore."
This gives them an opportunity to think and decide if the offer is worth it or not.

This would be an additional chore, not one that they are already responsible for but that is going to take their time. Maybe it is raking the leaves in the backyard or cleaning the basement. Something that is age-specific and appropriate.

You want to teach them to think and say,

"Okay. Well, I have to invest my time because I don't have money,"

and then be able to equate that with money than you can save some time. If you don't have money, well then you have to take and invest more time.

ASSIGNMENT #17

Look for opportunities to teach your child about money and what things cost. Let them know that things are not **FREE** and that they don't just **GET** anything they want anytime they want it.

I have created a job list that you can download to give some ideas of how to set a system like this up for your family.

Would you like to get free updates and some _COOL_ gifts?
I am constantly working on new skills and adding techniques to my toolkit.
When I add something to this book, you will get it for free. Just visit:

http://DennyStrecker.com/confidencebook-bonus

CHAPTER 18. LEARN RESPONSIBILITY

"Hold yourself responsible for a higher standard than anybody expects of you. Never excuse yourself." - **Henry Ward Beecher**

THE BAT AND THE WEASELS

Bat who fell upon the ground and was caught by a Weasel pleaded to be spared his life. The Weasel refused, saying that he was by nature the enemy of all birds. The Bat assured him that he was not a bird, but a mouse, and thus was set free. Shortly afterwards the Bat again fell to the ground and was caught by another Weasel, whom he likewise entreated not to eat him. The Weasel said that he had a special hostility to mice. The Bat assured him that he was not a mouse, but a bat, and thus a second time escaped.

RESPONSIBILITY

Being able to teach your child to be responsible is probably one of the biggest reasons that parents bring their children to me. How many times have you said to yourself as a parent,

"I wish my child would be more responsible."

As parents, we certainly want our children to grow up to be responsible. This includes taking responsibility for their actions, commitments, outcomes and decisions.

When your child was born, you assumed full responsibility for them. Then over the next 18 years, your job, your responsibility is to gradually turn that responsibility back to them by teaching them how to take care of things themselves. Teaching your child to be responsible takes time and attention and every bit of responsibility you give your child must come with a tremendous amount of instruction and supervision. To raise a responsible child, you must be prepared to teach, remind and inspect over and over a zillion times if necessary. You must be prepared to do it without becoming frustrated, impatient or resentful.

What we have got is a model that you are able to follow to teach your child on how to handle responsibility. There are four basic steps:

#1 - You assign a task, you teach what is expected and how to meet those expectations.

#2 - You provide an opportunity to work on that particular task.

#3 - You inspect and you provide constructive feedback. The emphasis needs to be on the constructive feedback.

#4 - Reach your goal. Celebrate and set a new goal.

Too often parents talk sarcastically to their kids. When they turn into teenagers and they have heard that for the past 12 to 15 years and it starts coming back at you, it is going to be razor sharp and it is going to be polished and it is going to be very difficult to deal with. You taught that skill to them if you speak to them that way.

The next point I want you to think about is not using the word "but" in sentences. Anytime somebody uses the word "but" it means,

"Ignore what I've said before. Here is my excuse for not doing it."

If you give your child a particular task and then you say,

"Well, that looks good but if you do this it'll be better."

How To Double Your Child's Self-Confidence in Just 30 Days

There is nothing constructive, it is just negative. Your child is not going to remember you said it looks good. They are only going to remember that you were not happy. Remove the word "but" and make it constructive criticism.

Ok, back to our model. What do you do when your child is not successful? You continue with step number three, going back with constructive criticism. If your child's results were not quite successful, then you go all the way back to Step #1. You assign the task and you teach what is expected and how to meet those expectations.

Don't throw in the towel and say,

"Forget it, I'll do it myself."

If you do, you are destroying your child's self-confidence and self-esteem. You are telling them that you don't believe in them or that they can do the task correctly. That is **NEVER** a message you want to send to your child.

Start to implement the responsibility model today. If your child's efforts were not successful, don't take away the responsibility. It just means your child needs more teaching and more feedback. You must be patient and supportive. If you appear disappointed or impatient, your child will become discouraged and resentful.

If you don't have a responsible child, think about it. Some parents say,

"Okay, yeah. They are five, they are seven, they are 10, they are not responsible. So what?"

How many stories do you hear about adults still living at home at 30-years-old, 35-year-olds, or older. They have never been able to go out and live by themselves because they are not responsible enough to do so.

I don't know any parent that has a child saying,

"You know what? I'm looking forward to that time when my child is 40 and still in the house."

As much as you love them and as much as you want them to be part of your life, you want them to be able to stand on their own two feet.

Being able to teach them responsibility is going to be important but it is a huge mistake to assume that the children are going to grow up to be responsible adults without coaching and help. You have got to be diligent, use this model, don't become frustrated or give up. Giving up is not an option. You stick with it and your child will learn to handle all types of responsibility effectively.

It is not always simple because you are going to catch yourself forgetting or using those negative words. That is OK. When you forget, make sure you catch it the next time. If you start to become negative, stop, take a breath, and change your vocabulary. Strive for improvement not perfection - sound familiar?

ASSIGNMENT #18

One of the greatest gifts you can give your child is the ability to be responsible. As with all valuable things, this is a skill and needs to be taught to them until they get it. That means over and over again for months or even years.

Create a Responsibility List. This is a list of things you want your child to be able to do on their own. Next, number each item in order of preference. What is the #1 thing in your opinion that your child needs to learn? Then #2, #3 and so on. Now, go back to number #1 and create a plan on how you are going to teach that skill to your child. A great place to start would be in our previous chapter and have the kids make their bed.

You can make the list as long as you like. Here are some of things I think are important: cleaning your room, picking up after yourself, using a vacuum, doing laundry, how to make breakfast, getting your own beverages, getting your own snacks, how to cook, managing money and getting up every morning on time. This is by no means a complete list, but certainly is enough to keep you busy for a couple years.

Would you like to get free updates and some _COOL_ gifts?
I am constantly working on new skills and adding techniques to my toolkit.
When I add something to this book, you will get it for free. Just visit:

http://DennyStrecker.com/confidencebook-bonus

CHAPTER 19. GIVE UNCONDITIONAL LOVE

"Being deeply loved by someone gives you strength, while loving someone deeply gives you courage." - **Lao Tzu**

THE LION AND THE THREE BULLS

Three Bulls for a long time pastured together. A Lion lay in ambush in the hope of making them his prey, but was afraid to attack them while they kept together. Having at last by guileful speeches succeeded in separating them, he attacked them without fear as they fed alone, and feasted on them one by one at his own leisure..

UNCONDITIONAL LOVE

Giving unconditional love is both verbal and physical. You hear people all of the time say,

"My parents never told me that they loved me."

Or,

" They never hugged me, our family are not huggers."

That is just a crime in my opinion. All right, I may be a little biased. I am very big about giving out hugs to people - especially if they are having a bad day. Anybody that asks me for one can certainly gets it. I am more than happy to oblige for a couple of reasons. First, because it just gives the person that sense that I care - which I do. Second, it releases a hormone called Oxytocin (which is called the "love hormone") in both me AND the other person. So it makes it a win-win event because we both feel happier now!

There is so much power in a hug. As a matter of fact, I was watching the movie "Santa Clause 3" one night. It wasn't a great movie, so you don't have

How To Double Your Child's Self-Confidence in Just 30 Days

to go out and rent it right away. In the very end of the movie, the little girl gives Jack Frost (who is obviously Mr. Cold) a hug and it just warms him up, and it changes his whole life. So seeing stuff like that is very powerful.

So if you are not a hugger, try to start. It can be a pat on the back, or a high five, or even a handshake. Any personal contact is a good start and will start to release more Oxytocin into your system. So hugging is what works for me and it is what I enjoy. If it works for you, great! If not, find something else that works.

The two most important things about this process are:

#1 - Tell your children, your spouse, your family, your friends how important they are to you, and tell them that you love them, and tell them regularly. Not just once in awhile.

#2 - Show it and make it physical. If it is a high five, or a hug, whatever works for you fine. Find your thing.

How To Double Your Child's Self-Confidence in Just 30 Days

ASSIGNMENT #19

I have created a worksheet of 100 Ways to Positively Reinforce your child. You can download this worksheet at my bonus website listed below. Then, get to work on using all 100 phrases or sayings, and see how long it takes you. Then start again and try and beat your best time.

Would you like to get free updates and some _COOL_ gifts?
I am constantly working on new skills and adding techniques to my toolkit. When I add something to this book, you will get it for free. Just visit:

http://DennyStrecker.com/confidencebook-bonus

CHAPTER 20. ACTIVELY LISTEN

*"We have two ears and one mouth so that
we can listen twice as much as we speak."* - **Epictetus**

THE NORTH WIND AND THE SUN

The North Wind and the Sun disputed as to which was the most powerful, and agreed that he should be declared the victor who could first strip a wayfaring man of his clothes. The North Wind first tried his power and blew with all his might, but the keener his blasts, the closer the Traveler wrapped his cloak around him, until at last, resigning all hope of victory, the Wind called upon the Sun to see what he could do. The Sun suddenly shone out with all his warmth. The Traveler no sooner felt his genial rays than he took off one garment after another, and at last, fairly overcome with heat, undressed and bathed in a stream that lay in his path.

ACTIVELY LISTEN

Actively listen to your child, is an important skill to develop so they know that you are paying attention to them and what they are saying. Parents too often say,

"Yeah, yep, uh-huh, ok, great." Etc.

Instead of that, look at your child, eye to eye, when they are talking. If you ever watch me working with kids, the first thing you will notice is that I squat down to their level because I want to connect with them. I do not like a child looking up at me when they talk. That puts me in a position of superiority. It makes me look big and scary. I do not want to look big and scary to any child. I want them to feel happy and safe around me so I do everything I can to create that atmosphere.

So make sure you squat down to your child's level so you can make eye contact with them while they are talking. They may be bashful or shy, they might look down or they might look away. That is telling you that they lack confidence in themselves. Start to create opportunities for them to practice making eye contact. If you see your child is not looking at you, you can say something like,

"Hey! look at this?" and then make the silliest face you can.

Do something like that enough times, and your child will **WANT** to look at you just to see what you might do next.

I get kids running into my karate school all the time just to tell me something they did that day. They wanted to share it with me, and if I take that two seconds to stop whatever I am doing and speak to them, it makes their day. Whatever they have to tell me probably is not "earth shattering", but it means the world to that child, so it is important to me.

You need to take the time, even if it is just two seconds, or even if it is 10 minutes, to actively listen. Give them good eye contact and your undivided attention. Then ask them questions or add to their story and you will watch them light up like crazy.

ASSIGNMENT #20

Start to participate in conversations with your child. Ask them questions about what they are telling you so they can tell you even more about it. You can score all kinds of "cool" points if you just add something to their story and then let them run with it.

It is easy to get bogged down with the day to day stuff and forget that your child NEEDS your attention. But by giving them just a few minutes of your time each day, they will be happy for a lifetime.

Go ask your child right now, *"What are you doing?"*

Would you like to get free updates and some _COOL_ gifts?
I am constantly working on new skills and adding techniques to my toolkit.
When I add something to this book, you will get it for free. Just visit:

http://DennyStrecker.com/confidencebook-bonus

Chapter 21. Making Every Experience a Lesson in Learning

"There are no secrets to success. It is the result of preparation, hard work, and learning from failure." - **Colin Powell**

The Fisherman

Some Fishermen were out trawling their nets. Perceiving them to be very heavy, they danced about for joy and supposed that they had taken a large catch. When they had dragged the nets to the shore they found but few fish: the nets were full of sand and stones, and the men were beyond measure cast down so much at the disappointment which had befallen them, but because they had formed such very different expectations. One of their company, an old man, said, "Let us cease lamenting, my mates, for, as it seems to me, sorrow is always the twin sister of joy; and it was only to be looked for that we, who just now were over-rejoiced, should next have something to make us sad.

Lesson Learned

Parents should make every situation a positive learning experience. It is so easy to be negative, to yell, to scream, to put down, or to punish. When that happens, you missed an opportunity to help your child learn something.

Okay, you messed up.

So what?

All right, fix it. Here is how. By making it into a learning experience, you are going to increase the chances that this does not happen again. If you yell and scream at them, it is probably going to happen again. It is just a matter of when. That is because children forget, and when they forget, they make the same silly mistake again.

This can be tough. If you are in the heat of the moment, and they have just done something, you may yell at them. I remember when I was young, computers and the internet just came out. My dad worked for IBM. He had just spent hours and hours of work on the computer that was connected to the phone line. He told us not to pick up the phone but I forgot. Well, I picked up the phone to make a call and the connection was lost. He lost all of the work that he had done for the past two hours.. Needless to say, he was not pleased. He yelled at me for quite a while.

How can you make something a positive learning experience? Take your time, take a step back, and take a deep breath. Then, say to your child;

"Okay, I'm very upset. Let me calm down before we talk about this."

There is nothing saying that you have got to discipline and work with your child right away. Try to find a positive solution.

ASSIGNMENT #21

Make it a point to find opportunities to teach your child something. If you stay on the lookout, you will begin to see how many there are in a day. Maybe it is explaining WHY something is done this way or that way. Maybe it is teaching them something they did not know about. Maybe it is simply a chance to ask them questions. It does not matter WHAT the opportunity is, just make sure you take it.

Would you like to get free updates and some _COOL_ gifts?
I am constantly working on new skills and adding techniques to my toolkit. When I add something to this book, you will get it for free. Just visit:

http://DennyStrecker.com/confidencebook-bonus

CHAPTER 22. BECOME AN EXPERT

"An investment in knowledge pays the best interest.."
- Benjamin Franklin

HERCULES AND THE WAGONER

A carter was driving a wagon along a country lane, when the wheels sank down deep into a rut. The rustic driver, stupefied and aghast, stood looking at the wagon, and did nothing but utter loud cries to Hercules to come and help him. Hercules, it is said, appeared and thus addressed him: "Put your shoulders to the wheels, my man. Goad on your bullocks, and never more pray to me for help, until you have done your best to help yourself, or depend upon it you will henceforth pray in vain.

BE THE EXPERT

What I mean by become an expert is to get involved in what your kids are doing. A lot of activities have what I call "drop off" parents. Parents that will drop their kid off and then say,

"Okay they are in class, great. I have got an hour so I can go do something else."

On occasion this may be necessary, especially if you have more than one child. But there are some parents that do this every single class - day in, day out, week after week, month after month. They have no idea what their child is doing, what they are learning or the benefits that they are getting from the activity.

Don't be that type of parent! Get involved in what your kids are doing. Become a part of it, and then become the "expert" so that you can help them when they need it. You will also be able to spend quality time with them because you will be able to answer their questions and help.

95
How To Double Your Child's Self-Confidence in Just 30 Days

A great example is homework. Parents all the time say,

"Well I can't help you with Algebra because I always stunk at it. I was terrible."

Well, you have a child now. It is time to get good at it. You have got a second chance so sit down with them, learn Algebra or whatever the subject might be. Become an expert so that your child sees you as the "go to" source when it comes to the answers.

ASSIGNMENT #22

Start with a single subject. Is your child into Minecraft or Skylanders? Start to learn about the game, the characters, the goals, etc. so you can participate in the conversation. Why not even play the game a little? Let them teach you how to play so THEY can feel like the expert.

Would you like to get free updates and some *COOL* gifts?
I am constantly working on new skills and adding techniques to my toolkit. When I add something to this book, you will get it for free. Just visit:

http://DennyStrecker.com/confidencebook-bonus

CHAPTER 23. LEAD A HEALTHY LIFESTYLE

THE ANTS AND THE GRASSHOPPER

The Ants were spending a fine winter's day drying grain collected in the summertime. A Grasshopper, perishing with famine, passed by and earnestly begged for a little food. The Ants inquired of him, "Why did you not treasure up food during the summer?' He replied, "I had not leisure enough. I passed the days in singing." They then said in derision: "If you were foolish enough to sing all the summer, you must dance supperless to bed in the winter.

HEALTHY LIFESTYLE

Parents need to teach their child how to have a healthy lifestyle. I have added a couple of stories to the bonus website for you to read. Obesity is a big problem today. It is reaching epidemic proportions.

Let me give you two rules to help you get your child moving and active - especially during the summer months.

The first rule is:

Reading time should equal TV, video game, or computer time.

If your child wants to spend an hour in front of the TV, no problem. They need to read a book for an hour. If they want to spend all day Saturday in front of the TV, then they need to spend all day some other day reading a book. By setting these limits, you are going to get rid of those couch potatoes.

Does it have to be reading time? No. If you have a young child, it could be playtime. You need to be outside playing for every minute that you are inside watching TV. So you can tweak this to fit your child's needs.

"Well I'm not watching TV. I'm playing on my new WII or my PlayStation, or Nintendo."

That's TV time.

"But I'm playing on the computer/tablet."

Anything with a screen is TV time.

The second rule for your children, and you as a matter of fact because your a role model for your children, is that they should go to bed at the same time every day, seven days a week, 365 days a year, and should also get up at the same time every day of the year.

Why is this important?

You, and your children, are going to get a lot more done. Can you imagine how many Saturdays and/or Sundays are wasted by your teenagers sleeping until 1:00pm? I hear this all the time. My martial arts class for the kids is at 11:00 a.m. and 12:00 p.m. and I get sleepy eyes walking in the door because their parents pulled them out of bed to come to karate at 12:00pm.

I am up at 8:00am and at the school by 9:00 so I can get ready for classes. So I have been up for hours and I have gotten a lot of things done.

This is a *goal,* it is not a **rule**, there is a difference. Your goal is to do this every day of the year. If you miss one is that okay? Absolutely! We are not perfect, we are human beings. So you want to be able to find a happy medium and get back on track as soon as you can.

ASSIGNMENT #23

Start to find ways to improve your lifestyle for the entire family. Make a list and decide which item is the most important to start and do just that one. Then move on to the next when you believe the first one is solid and in place.

Would you like to get free updates and some _COOL_ gifts?
I am constantly working on new skills and adding techniques to my toolkit. When I add something to this book, you will get it for free. Just visit:

http://DennyStrecker.com/confidencebook-bonus

Chapter 24. Give Your Child Chores

"Hold yourself responsible for a higher standard than anybody expects of you. Never excuse yourself."
- Henry Ward Beecher

The Traveler And His Dog

A traveler about to set out on a journey saw his Dog stand at the door stretching himself. He asked him sharply: "Why do you stand there gaping? Everything is ready but you, so come with me instantly." The Dog, wagging his tail, replied: "O, master! I am quite ready; it is you for whom I am waiting.

Your Child Should Have Chores

Every family I see where the children do not have any chores is a family in struggle. Again, the children start to feel that they are owed everything and that the world revolves around them; and I can see why.

If you look back in the ancient Egyptian times with the pharaohs or any history where there was a king or a monarch of any sort and they're waited on hand and foot, there becomes a sense of entitlement. Why wouldn't kids pick that up? If I can yell downstairs, "Mom, get me a soda!" and you bring it to him, well you're going to start creating that situation. Certainly making sure, again, chores need to be age-appropriate and at that point, then you've got to make a decision on what you think is appropriate.

Again, we've got two schools of thought. You've got some of the parents that would fall more on the hardcore, a military side and so at that point, it becomes they're very strict and it's got to be done exactly this way or else it's wrong. Then, you've got the exact opposite of, "Well, it's easier for me to do it than them so I'm not going to bother giving them any chores because it'll take twice as long." After I get done smacking you upside the head with

100
How To Double Your Child's Self-Confidence in Just 30 Days

that thinking, basically what you're getting to or what I try to approach is you want a short-term pain for a long-term gain.

I would rather work with a child at whatever age now for three to six months to teach them this particular habit, whatever that habit might be, which is going to last the rest of their life than to ignore it and have to do this extra work and extra task myself for the next five, 10, 15 years. Then at that point, once they move out on their own, they're still not going to have that skill so they're still going to be coming back and trying to rely on it. A perfect example is when kids go off to college. We all joke about it here, at least in the United States.

When kids go out to college, they come home for two things ... Well, sometimes three but basically: money and more important, laundry. I don't know any college student, and I'm sure they're out there, I just haven't met them yet, that hasn't come home with that big huge bag of dirty clothes that says, "Great, I'm home. Here, do my laundry." Even if you don't do it, if they just bring it home and they do it themselves, that's one step better. Certainly, if you start young, give the kids or your children just a small chore.

If it's setting the table for dinner or emptying the dishwasher or putting your clothes in the clothes bin, anything like that so that they realize that as part of this family, your responsibility is to take care of these chores and we all have chores. Then, they start to realize that the family is important and for everybody to participate as a group is what's going to make the family that much stronger.

Assignment #24

Create a list of chores for your child to complete each week. You can attach rewards if you like for completed sheets.

Would you like to get free updates and some _COOL_ gifts?
I am constantly working on new skills and adding techniques to my toolkit. When I add something to this book, you will get it for free. Just visit:

http://DennyStrecker.com/confidencebook-bonus

How To Double Your Child's Self-Confidence in Just 30 Days

Chapter 25. Putting It All Together

"A leader is one who knows the way, goes the way, and shows the way."
- John C. Maxwell

The Dog And The Shadow

A Dog, crossing a bridge over a stream with a piece of flesh in his mouth, saw his own shadow in the water and took it for that of another Dog, with a piece of meat double his own in size. He immediately let go of his own, and fiercely attacked the other Dog to get his larger piece from him. He thus lost both: that which he grasped at in the water, because it was a shadow; and his own, because the stream swept it away.

Where Do I Begin?

It is easy to become overwhelmed with all of this information and end up not doing anything.

DON'T let that happen!

Make it a point to add something to your parenting arsenal at least once a month. Be ready to stick with it for at least three weeks. 90% of people give up 10% away from their goal. Read that again...

Don't throw in the towel and fall into the trap where you say to yourself,

"This isn't working!"

If you hang in there, success is very likely around the next corner. You just have to keep your eye on the goal and remain vigilant.

The way I approach each situation is I believe I have 2 options:

How To Double Your Child's Self-Confidence in Just 30 Days

#1 - I can continue to work on this situation and the child will get it - eventually.

#2 - Give up

#2 is **NEVER** an option to me. So, I continue to work and help the child any way I can.

This mindset allows me to remain calm and not to get frustrated because I know I am in it for the long haul. However long it takes. Because anything else is not fair to the child. I will always give each and every child my 100% best.

If you keep the end in mind, you will be better able to handle the short term struggles that are bound to come up. Frustration develops when you lose sight of your goal and feel "stuck". To prevent from feeling stuck, keep moving forwards. Even if it is just a crawl. Stick to your guns and you will be happy that you did.

How To Double Your Child's Self-Confidence in Just 30 Days

ASSIGNMENT #25

Take a deep breath, relax, and think about what you believe is the most important skill you want your child to learn. Then, go back, read that chapter again, and start there.

Just take one skill at a time and begin to implement. After several weeks, pick the next and add that to your plan. Before you know it, you will see some really positive results happening and will want to keep going.

Would you like to get free updates and some _COOL_ gifts?
I am constantly working on new skills and adding techniques to my toolkit.
When I add something to this book, you will get it for free. Just visit:

http://DennyStrecker.com/confidencebook-bonus

ABOUT THE AUTHOR

Denny Strecker teaches children the Life Skills necessary to lead a happy and successful life so that their parents **NEVER** have to wonder or worry about them. He has helped thousands of children earn better grades, learn how to lead a group, and how to set and reach goals that others only dream about.

Denny owns and operates his karate school for the past 25 years which is located in Troy Michigan. He has hundreds of students come to his classes weekly to work on their Life Skills and Development so they can do better in school and prepare for the real world.

Denny has spent the past 25 years studying child development and how to become the best teacher. Thousands of hours studying neuroscience, age specific training, age appropriate development and game theory.

He has used his classroom as his laboratory to see what things work (and what things don't work) hundreds of times to get the best results possible. Things that worked, he used again. Things that did not, got thrown out. Today, he has the most effective teaching system available for children ages 4 to 15.

Denny is originally from Troy, Michigan and it was a great day when he was able to move his karate school back to his hometown in 2014.

He has a Golden doodle named Yoshi who is his best friend and they hang out on the couch and watch movies and spend a lot of time at the park playing.

You can get more information from the sources below:

Podcast: http://dennystrecker.libsyn.com
YouTube: https://www.youtube.com/user/karatefit Facebook:
https://www.facebook.com/denny.strecker Twitter:
http://www.Twitter.com/DSKTroy
Google+: https://plus.google.com/+DennyStrecker
Blog: http://dennystrecker.com/blog/

Amazon Author Page: http://www.amazon.com/author/dennystrecker

How To Double Your Child's Self-Confidence in Just 30 Days

HIRE DENNY TO SPEAK AT YOUR EVENT!

Book Denny Strecker as your Keynote Speaker and You're Guaranteed to Make Your Event Highly Entertaining and Unforgettable!

For over two decades, Denny Strecker has been educating, entertaining and helping parents build and grow their skills to raise healthy and happy children.

His story includes owning and operating his martial arts school since 1992 where he has been able to practice and develop the tools needed to help children grow into the best versions of themselves. He has found the "secrets" to getting children to listen better, focus, set and complete goals and become leaders. After spending twenty-five years perfecting his skills, he is now sharing his best kept "secrets" with parents so they can benefit too.

His unique style inspires, empowers and entertains audiences while giving them the tools and strategies they need and want to help their children develop into great adults.

For more info, visit www.DennyStrecker.com/speaking or call (248) 687-8641.

ONE LAST THING...

If you enjoyed this book or found it useful I would be very grateful if you would post a short review on Amazon. Your support really does make a difference and I read all the reviews personally so I can get your feedback and make this book even better.

If you would like to leave a review then all you need to do is click the review link on this book's page on Amazon here:

https://www.amazon.com/review/create-review/ref=cm_cr_dp_d_wr_but_top?ie=UTF8&channel=glance-detail&asin=B071XPBG46#

Thanks again for your support!